usborne

Dressing-up Sticke[r]
Nativity Play

Illustrated by Kay Widdowson
Designed by Claire Ever
Words by Felicity Brooks

These children and their friends are putting on a Nativity play.
Use the stickers to help dress them in their costumes.

A long time ago Mary and Joseph had to go to the village of Bethlehem. Mary was expecting a baby.

Narrato

Joseph

Mary

In Bethlehem, Mary and Joseph went to an inn.

Innkeeper

Innkeeper's Wife

Mary	I'm so tired.
Joseph	Can we stay here?
Innkeeper	No, there's no room.
Wife	But you can stay in the stable.

That night Mary's baby was born.

Cow

Donkey

Mary	We will call him Jesus.
Joseph	Let's make his bed in this manger.
Cow	Moo!
Sheep	Baa!

Sheep

In the hills above Bethlehem some shepherds were taking care of their sheep.

Shepherd 1

Shepherd 2

Shepherd 3

Shepherd 1	What's that bright light?
Shepherd 2	I'm scared.
Shepherd 3	Me too.
Dog	Woof.

Suddenly a lovely angel appeared.

Angel

Dog

Angel   Don't be afraid. I have great news.
         A baby has been born who is the Son of God.
         You'll find him in a stable.

Soon the sky was full of beautiful
shining angels.

8

Sheep, Donkey and Cow (pages 4 and 5)

Sheep

Donkey

Cow

Baby Jesus

Shepherds, Dog and Angel (pages 6 and 7)

Shepherd 1

Shepherd 2

Dog

Angel

Angels (pages 8 and 9)

Angels

Three Kings (pages 10 and 11)

King 1

King 2

King 3

Star

Gifts for Baby Jesus (pages 12 and 13)

Gold

Myrrh

Frankincense

Narrator

Nativity scene (pages 14 and 15)

Mary

Joseph

Baby Jesus

Shepherd

Shepherd

Cow

Sheep

King

Shepherd

King

Star

King

Away in a manger (page 16)

Handbells

Drumsticks

Drum

Harp

Tambourine

Recorder

Angels

Angels	Glory to God and Peace on Earth!
Shepherd 1	We must tell everyone about this.
Shepherd 2	Let's go!

Far away, three wise men saw a bright star moving across the sky. They started to follow it.

King 2

King 1

| 3 Kings (singing) | We three kings of Orient are, Bearing gifts we travel so far. Field and fountain, moor and mountain, Following yonder star. |

Star

King 3

The shepherds visited the baby in the stable.

Shepherd 1	An angel told us to come.
Shepherd 3	We have brought a lamb as a present.
Mary	Thanks.

And at last the three kings arrived too.

Narrator

King 1	Here is my gift for Jesus, a casket of gold.
King 2	Here is mine, some sweet-smelling frankincense.
King 3	And I bring some myrrh, a precious spice from faraway lands.
Joseph	Thanks.

And that was the story of the very first
Christmas, a long, long time ago.

Everyone (singing) Away in a manger, no crib for a bed.
The little Lord Jesus lay down his sweet head.
The stars in the bright sky looked down where he lay.
The little Lord Jesus, asleep on the hay.

16